Noah
& the
Mighty Ark

RHONDA GOWLER GREENE

PICTURES BY
SANTIAGO COHEN

zonderkidz

zonderkidz
The children's group
of Zondervan

www.zonderkidz.com

Noah & the Mighty Ark
Copyright © 2007 by Rhonda Gowler Greene
Illustrations © 2007 by Santiago Cohen

Requests for information should be addressed to:
Grand Rapids, Michigan 49530

Library of Congress Cataloging-in-Publication Data

Green, Rhonda Gowler
    Noah & the mighty ark / by Rhonda Gowler Greene.
       p. cm.
    ISBN-13: 978-0-310-71097-4 (printed hardcover)
    ISBN-10: 0-310-71097-9 (printed hardcover)
    1. Noah's Ark–Juvenile literature.
    I. Title: Noah and the mighty ark. II. Title.
  BS658.G74 2007
  222'.1109505–dc22   2006005636

Editor: Amy De Vries
Art direction & design: Al Cetta

The body text for this book is set in Plantin Regular.

Printed in China

07 08 09 10 • 10 9 8 7 6 5 4 3 2 1

God saw how corrupt the earth had become. So God said to Noah, "Make yourself an ark of cypress wood. You are to bring into the ark two of all living creatures ..."
Taken from Genesis 6:12-19

For my daughter, Lianna, who loves all animals, little or big—RGG

With love to Ethel, Diego, Isabel—and all our pets: cats, dogs,
finches, fishes, turtles, and hamsters—PA'

God said,
"I will find
one good man,
strong and kind."

He found Noah,
said to him,
"Build an ark
   and rooms within."

Then God said,
"When you're through,
bring the creatures two
   by two."

So Noah did.
He built a boat
lined with pitch so it would float.

It stood tall
beneath the sun,
but Noah knew he wasn't done.

His sons brought water,
seed, and hay.
They filled the ark
   by night and day.

Then, he called the creatures
two by two—
the elephant and kangaroo,

the crocodile,
the chimpanzee,
the busy *buzzing* bumblebee,

the tiny gnat,

the BIG, BLACK BEAR.

From far and wide, he called each pair

that crept or crawled
or hopped or flew
or stomped or tromped, or s-s-slithered
too.

Yes, every creature
crowded in
and filled that ark
up to the brim!

While up above
that giant ark,
the sky was growing
very dark ...

Then lightning *flashed!*
and thunder *ROARED!*
When all were in ...

God shut the door.

And so the rain
began—*plip-plop!*
a rain that seemed to never stop.

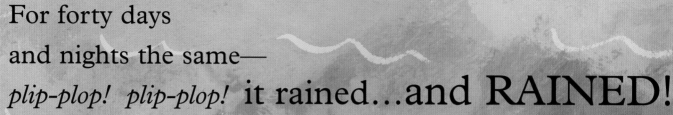

For forty days
and nights the same—
plip-plop! plip-plop! it rained…and RAINED!

The water s-w-e-l-l-e-d
to a great height
and covered everything in sight.

Those creatures, cramped
and squeezed inside,
huddled on that rocky ride.

Some *sh-sh-shivered.*
Some were filled with fear.
But Noah gently drew them near.

Then ...

Whoosh! wind filled the sky,
made land turn dry,
and finally ...

the sun appeared.

And Ararat,
a mountain steep,
became a perch from waters deep.

Then, a fine white dove
sent on its way
returned with hope one sun-kissed day.

And creatures
in that mighty ark
all lined up and disembarked.

They crept. They crawled.
They hopped. They flew.
They left that huge ark
two by two.

Noah told
each one goodbye.
Then God said,
    "Now multiply."

While in the sky,
a rainbow sign,
God's promise, still …
    to all mankind.